KINGDOM CLASSIFICATION

MOLDS, MUSHROOMS & OTHER

FUNGI

By Steve Parker

First published in the United States in 2009 by
Compass Point Books
A Capstone Imprint
151 Good Counsel Drive
P.O. Box 669
Mankato, MN 56002-0669

KINGDOM CLASSIFICATION—FUNGI
was produced by

David West Children's Books
7 Princeton Court
55 Felsham Road
London SW15 1AZ

Designer: Rob Shone
Editors: Gail Bushnell, Anthony Wacholtz
Page Production: Bobbie Nuytten

Creative Director: Joe Ewest
Art Director: LuAnn Ascheman-Adams
Editorial Director: Nick Healy
Managing Editor: Catherine Neitge

Library of Congress Cataloging-in-Publication Data
Parker, Steve, 1952–
  Molds, mushrooms & other fungi / by Steve Parker.
    p. cm.—(Kingdom classifications)
  Includes index.
  ISBN 978-0-7565-4223-8 (library binding)
  1. Fungi—Juvenile literature.
I. Title. II. Title: Molds, mushrooms and other fungi.
III. Series: Parker, Steve, 1952– Kingdom classifications.
  QK603.5.P36 2009
  579.5—dc22   2009010749

Visit Compass Point Books on the Internet at
www.capstonepub.com

PHOTO CREDITS :
Abbreviations: t-top, m-middle, b-bottom, r-right,
l-left, c-center.

Cover & 14m, iStockphoto/L. Nagy; 4–5, David Coder; 8l, 8–9,
41t, 42t, 43br, CDC/Dr. Libero Ajello; 8b, iStockphoto/Tomasz
Kopalski; 8t, iStockphoto/Mikael Damkier; 9tl, 20b, Jason
Hollinger; 10tl, 15tl, 15tr, Nathan Wilson; 10r, Archenzo; 10b,
Scott Bauer; 11, Eric Steinert; 12t, Wikimedia/Smardz
Sto kowaty; 12m, Jeff Nagy; 13tr, R. R. Smith; 13m, Carolina
Biological Supply Company; 13b, Matt Wharton; 14br, 18m,
23tl, 23tr, 30r, 31ml, Jean-Pol Grandmont; 15c, Clemson
University/USDA Cooperative Extension Slide Series; 15l, Joseph
O'Brien/USDA Forest Service; 16t, TK Edens; 16m, Rosemary
Winnall; 16b, Nino Barbieri; 17bl, Richard Packwood; 18bl,
Tony Wills; 19t, Josef F. Stuefer; 19ml, Tim McCormack; 19mr,
Tomasz Przechlewski; 19b, Snowmanradio; 20t, Karamell; 20m,
James Lindsey; 21tl, Retama; 21mr, Marty Cordano; 22l,
Andreas Tille; 22tr, bart; 22mr, Paul A. Mistretta/USDA Forest
Service; 22br, Eric Steinert; 24t, Andrew Dunn; 24r, Systematic
Mycology and Microbiology Laboratory, Agricultural Research
Service, USDA; 24b, Microscan; 25ml, 28br, 34l, 36r, 43bm,
OSF/Dennis Kunkel; 25tl, backpackphotography; 25tr, Michael
Kensinger; 25b, Peter Halasz; 26t, London Scientific Films; 27b,
Ism; 28t, Brian Michelsen; 28ml, Graham D. Schuster; 28bl,
Walter Siegmund; 29ml, Dean Biggins, U.S. Fish and Wildlife
Service; 29tr, Think outside the box; 29mr, Jens Buurgaard
Nielsen; 30bl, pfctdayelise; 30–31, Andrew Bossi; 31mr, David
Remahl; 32, Tony Wills; 33bl, Arria Belli; 33br, Severine
Meißner; 34mr, Nleamy; 36l, Steve Jurvetson; 36t, CDC/James
Gathany; 36bl, Namboori B. Raju/ Stanford University; 37t,
CDC/Janice Carr; 37m, C. James Webb; 37b, OSF/Maximilian
Stock Ltd; 38tr, Edward L. Barnard/Florida Department of
Agriculture and Consumer Services; 39tl, Tom Maack; 39ml,
stu_spivack; 39mr, Anthony De Lucca; 39br, Ken Hammond;
39b, Christine Stone; 40t, Ævar Arnfjörð Bjarmason; 40l, Dr.
David Midgley; 41m, Joel Mills; 41br, Forrest Brem; 41bl, 42m,
42br, CDC/Dr. Lucille K. Georg; 42bl, CDC/ Dr. Edwin P.
Ewing; 43mr, M. Renz; 45b, Onderwijsgek.

Every effort has been made to contact copyright
holders of any material reproduced in this book.
Any omissions will be rectified in subsequent
printings if notice is given to the publishers.

Front cover: Fly agaric toadstool
Opposite: Starfish stinkhorn fungus

KINGDOM CLASSIFICATION

MOLDS, MUSHROOMS & OTHER
FUNGI

Steve Parker

Compass Point Books ✦ Minneapolis, Minnesota

CONTENTS

INTRODUCTION

The world is full of living things, from tiny bugs and delicate flowers to giant trees, huge elephants, and massive whales. But nothing lives forever. Eventually all plants, animals, and other forms of life die. But what happens to them?

The answer: They become food for fungi. This kingdom of living things includes mushrooms, toadstools, molds, mildews, yeasts, and many others. Fungi are nature's recyclers. They feed by decaying, decomposing, and rotting old, dying, and dead plants and animals to obtain nourishment. As this happens, the fungi break down the once-living matter into simple, tiny pieces. These return to the soil and water, becoming nourishment for growing plants and animals.

MAKING MORE FUNGI

The most familiar parts of fungi, such as milk caps and honey fungus, are often called mushrooms or toadstools. But most fungi have other, larger parts, too. These are usually hidden in the soil or inside the bodies of animals and plants.

WHAT ARE FUNGI?

Fungi are neither plants nor animals. They form a separate kingdom of living things, grouped together by the way they obtain their food.

ONE OR MANY CELLS
Some fungi are microscopic and single-celled, each one a single living unit. Other fungi are multicelled, with a body made of thousands or millions of cells joined together. Some of the biggest fungi form a tangled network in the soil that stretches for hundreds of yards.

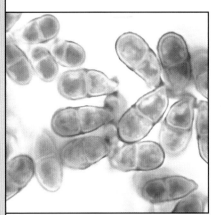

SPORES
Most fungi make microscopic spores that spread to new places and grow. The spores of Trichothecium cause pink rot in apples.

HOW FUNGI FEED
A fungus has no mouth and cannot eat pieces of food like a typical animal. It cannot trap and use sunlight energy like a green plant, either. Fungi absorb tiny particles of nutrients through their outer layer. It's like soaking up a nourishing soup through your skin.

FRUITING BODIES
The fruiting bodies of fungi— the mushrooms and toadstools— are the parts that produce and release the spores.

HARMFUL
The fungus Trichophyton (above) feeds on human skin, hair, and nails. It causes various kinds of infections, such as athlete's foot and ringworm.

MOLDS BUT NOT FUNGI

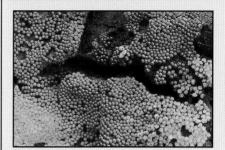

Yellow slime mold

Some kinds of fungi are known as molds. But not all molds are fungi. Water molds, called oomycetes, look like clumps of very fine pale hairs. They live in water, especially running water. Strange slime molds called mycetozoans can form jellylike lumps that slide along like slugs. The detailed structure of the cells from slime molds and water molds show that they are more closely related to the protist group than to fungi.

The dog vomit slime mold is a form of the scrambled egg slime mold (Fuligo septica).

GETTING MOLDY

When fungi grow on a living thing, or something that was once living, they often form patches of powder, fluff, or slime. On damp wallpaper (above) fungi feed on the paper fibers that were once tree wood, while an over-ripe apple (below) has several fungal growths.

TYPES OF CELLS

The cells of a fungus are eukaryotic. This means they have sheetlike membranes inside, enclosing structures such as the genetic material DNA in the nucleus—the cell's control center. Animal and plant cells are also eukaryotic. So are the living things called protists, which are usually single cells, like the amoeba. But the microbes called bacteria lack membranes inside and are known as prokaryotic.

PARTS OF A FUNGUS

The main bodies of most fungi do their work unseen, in places like the soil and within dead bodies. Only when fungi make spores do we notice them.

BEING BORN
An Amanita *emerges from its universal veil (right), a covering that protects the young mushroom. As the stalk grows, it leaves behind a torn fragment, the volva (above). Many species of* Amanita, *some deadly, have distinctive volvas.*

FRUITING BODY
The mushroom Agaricus campestris *has a fruiting body up to 4 inches (10 centimeters) across.*

FEED AND BREED
A typical fungus begins life as a microscopic spore. In a suitable damp place, the fungus sprouts a tangle of threads called the mycelium, which is the fungus' main body and feeding part. Later the fungus sends up fruiting bodies, usually known as mushrooms or toadstools, which are its breeding parts.

STUDYING FUNGI

The scientific study of mushrooms, molds, and other fungi is known as mycology. Experts on fungi are called mycologists. The study of fungal diseases is called mycopathology.

A mycologist checks fungi to be used as weed killers, infecting unwanted plants.

Annulus or ring (when present) is usually where the edge of the cap joins the stalk

CAP (PILEUS)

The top of the ripe fruiting body is the cap. It can be shaped like a wide, down-turned umbrella, a narrow upside-down cup, or a flat tabletop.

STALK (STIPE)

The stemlike stalk holds the cap above the soil or other surface where the mycelium is growing. This allows the spores to easily fall and spread.

BASAL CUP (VOLVA)

In some fungi, the edge of the stalk is joined to a baglike part at the base of the stalk called the volva.

MYCELIUM

The mycelium is a spreading network of thin threads called hyphae. These grow and lengthen in any direction where there are suitable conditions of moisture and nutrients. In total bulk, if the mycelium were all squeezed together, it would be many times larger than the fruiting body.

Basidium

GILLS

Many fungi have ridge-like gills called lamellae. The gills are arranged like wheel spokes. Their sides are covered by the hymenium layer with its spore-making parts.

SPORE-MAKERS

Spores are made by special cells on the hymenium. They are shaped like bags, sacks, clubs, or boxes, depending on the type of fungus. Basidia cells of a basidio-mycete fungus (inset, above left) have various shapes.

SPORES

Four spores are produced by each basidium cell.

HYPHAE

The hyphal threads make natural chemicals called digestive enzymes. These break down nearby substances, forming pieces so tiny that the hyphae can take them in and absorb them as food.

11

There are six to 10 main groups of fungi. They differ mainly in the way they produce their spores, rather than in fruiting body shape or color.

ASCOMYCETES

The ascomycetes are also known as sac fungi. They bear their spores in tiny structures called asci, which are shaped like bags, flasks, or pockets. They are the largest group of fungi, with more than 30,000 species, including morels, truffles, yeasts, and plant-infecting mildews.

MORELS

Morels have ridges and pits that look like nets or honeycombs. They are very tasty and prized for cooking.

ORANGES

Orange-peel fungus Aleuria *is a type of ascomycete.*

BRAINS AND TRUMPETS

Many fungi have names based on the similarity of their fruiting bodies to other objects. Yellow brain fungus Tremella *(left), a basidiomycete, appears in woods in the winter. Trumpet mushrooms such as* Pleurotus *(below) are farmed for food.*

JELLIES

Jelly fungi such as Auricularia *are basidiomycetes. They have a rubbery texture.*

BASIDIOMYCETES

Also called club fungi, these fungi make their spores in structures shaped like clubs, hammers, or baseball bats. There are almost 30,000 species, including common mushrooms, toadstools, brackets, puffballs, and earthstars.

HARD AND TOUGH

The outer walls of fungal cells are strengthened with chitin. This starch-based substance forms a strong, flexible, transparent case for the cell. Chitin is also found in insects and crustaceans, such as crabs and shrimp. The thick layers of chitin are strengthened with minerals. The chitin forms the animal's hard outer body casing.

Fungal cells and bugs are both protected by chitin.

MUTUAL FRIENDS

Fungi from several groups form growths known as mycorrhizae in and on plant roots. The fungus produces enzymes that dissolve nearby soil nutrients so the roots can absorb them. In return the plant gives the fungus a safe place to live. In clover (above) common types of glomeromycete fungi include Glomus *and* Gigaspora *(inset).*

SMALLER FUNGAL GROUPS

There are about 200 species of Glomeromycetes, and most live in a symbiosis, a beneficial partnership, with plants, such as clover, grasses, and orchids. They live in the roots and share nutrients with the plants.

Chytrid fungi make their spores in pot-shaped structures. There are about 1,000 species. A few cause diseases in animals and plants. Zygomycetes also number about 1,000 species. Many live in the soil or in rotting bodies of plants and animals.

MOLDY BREAD

Black bread mold Rhizopus *is a type of zygomycete fungus. Its hyphae form a pale fuzzy layer over bread, cakes, and similar foods (left). The darker areas are tiny spore-making parts, sporangia (above).*

LEGENDS AND TALES

Around the world, various kinds of fungi are featured in myths and folk tales. They are often linked to magic and spells.

THE ORIGINAL TOADSTOOL

The fly agaric mushroom, Amanita muscaria (right), is found in most regions and has a bright red cap with white spots. In some tales, this mushroom is part of witches' brews (above right).

LIVING IN THE DARK

Many fungi grow in dark, damp corners of buildings, shady woods, and other dimly lit places. Fungi are also associated with decay and disease because they thrive on the dying and dead. Sometimes fungi seem to spring up from nowhere during the night. In good conditions, a fruiting body can grow from a hidden mycelium and ripen in just a few hours.

FAIRY CAPS AND WITCH BUTTER

Small, delicate fungi are often linked to fairies, such as fairy caps (left), fairy cups, and fairy thimbles. Witches' butter is the common name for several jelly fungi, such as members of the Tremella group (right).

THE PRINCE MUSHROOM

Agaricus augustus is a "prince" among mushrooms. It's valued for its strong flavor, which makes it taste like almonds.

POISON POTIONS

Some tales have a scientific basis. The chemicals in certain fungi, when eaten, cause people to behave oddly, see or hear strange things, fall ill, or even die. No wonder molds, mushrooms, and toadstools were mixed up with witchcraft and wizardry.

CRAMP BALLS

Also called cramp balls, Daldinia concentrica is usually found on old ash trees.

HARMFUL MUSHROOMS

Fungi such as Psilocybin (right) contain harmful chemicals that, when eaten, affect the brain. People who have eaten this mushroom may experience hallucinations.

FAIRY RINGS (PIXIE RINGS)

People once wondered why certain fungi grew in ring patterns. They wondered whether the fungi sprang up where fairies or pixies had danced in a circle. Now we know that several types of mycelium fungi grow from a central area out through the soil as a widening circle. In favorable conditions, the outer edges produce fruiting bodies.

Marasmius *fairy mushrooms*

Ring mushrooms often appear together on grassy areas. As the mycelium grows over months or years, the ring gets larger.

FIELDS AND MEADOWS

O pen areas such as grasslands are good places to spot fungi, especially after rain has dampened the soil.

AFTER THE RAIN

All kinds of life need water to survive, but most grasslands thrive in fairly dry regions. After a rain shower, fungal mycelia often grow fast and sprout fruiting bodies rapidly. If they can make and release their spores quickly, the soil will still be damp when the spores land. This provides suitable conditions for spores to start growing during germination.

NO SUN

Unlike plants, fungi, such as meadow mushrooms (above) and parrot toadstools (left), do not need sunlight. They can grow in very dark places.

SPEEDY BREEDING

An open landscape, compared to sheltered woods, allows wind to spread fungal spores widely. Grassland soil is rich in nutrients, which the fungi absorb for speedy growth. However, they must finish their life cycle rapidly. As sunny, dry weather returns, they shrivel away.

HAIRY MANE

Also called shaggy ink-cap or hairy mane, Coprinus comatus has a scaly cap. It is found on roadsides and in lawns and stony areas.

PUFFBALLS

There are about 400 species of puffball fungi in the basidiomycete group. Their fruiting bodies begin like many other mushrooms and toadstools, pushing up from the soil. But they ripen into ball-shaped masses. Some are smaller than a pea. Others are larger than a beach ball. These balls release their spores as yellow or brown clouds when they dry out, when it rains, or when they are squeezed.

Giant puffballs, such as Calvatia gigantea *(left), can weigh more than 44 pounds (20 kilograms) and produce trillions of spores.*

Champignon, a name based on a French term for "mushroom," is given to various kinds of whitish or pale fungi that grow in fields and woods. Depending on where and how it grows, the same species may be called fairy ring champignon, field champignon, wood champignon, or moss champignon.

PARASOLS

The parasol mushroom Macrolepiota procera *is common on well-drained soil in fairly dry places. It can grow up to 16 inches (40 cm). Its cap and stalk often have ridged scales.*

Puffball Lycoperdon, *which grows on old wood, releases its spores in a cloudy mist.*

17

BROAD-LEAVED WOODS

The natural homes of many fungi are deciduous broad-leaved woodlands—especially as trees lose their leaves and die in the fall.

BACK TO THE SOIL

In woods and forests, the cooler, shorter days of autumn bring a steady fluttering of dying leaves. These are an important source of nutrients that are recycled into the soil. The roots will soak them up as the trees come back to life next spring. Tiny webs of mycelia spread over the leaf litter. Leaf loss means that as sunlight reaches the forest floor, fungi glow in a variety of sizes, shapes, and colors.

THRIVING FUNGI

As the leaf canopy disappears in autumn (above), fungi poke their fruiting bodies up through the leafy carpet. One of the biggest, best known, and tastiest types is Boletus edulis *(above left), known in various regions as cep, porcini, king bolete, and penny bun. Shiny and white, the porcelain or ice mushroom* Oudemansiella mucida *thrives mainly in beech woods.*

RUSSULAS

There are more than 700 species of red or brown Russula, *which are mostly mycorrhizal, growing among tree roots.*

CORALS

Bright-colored, upward-branched coral fungi are common in old, undisturbed woods.

EARTHSTARS

The earthstars (geastracea fungi) are close relatives of puffballs in the basidiomycete group. They are ball-shaped with almost no stalk. In dry weather, the outer layer curls around and protects the inside. In damp conditions, it splits and curls back like flower petals to reveal another ball shape, the spore container. This puffs out clouds of spores when jolted by rain, wind, or animals.

Earthstars grow to nearly 12 inches (30 cm) across.

HORRIBLE HONEY

The appearance of the honey fungus Armillaria *means a tree is dying. Black strands grow from the soil and roots up under the trunk bark, sending out fruiting bodies through cracks.*

BREAKING WOOD

Fungi also grow on tree trunks, broken branches, and fallen logs. They steadily digest the tough wood, making it soft and cracked. This allows beetles, ants, worms, and other bugs to tunnel inward. Fungal spores attach to the insects' bodies. They grow and continue to rot the wood from within. Soon the timber is decayed and crumbling, a new home for the decomposers.

NOT BIRD'S NESTS

The small "eggs" in bird's nest fungi such as Crucibulum *are spore containers called peridioles.*

FOREST FORAGERS

Fungi are food for many forest animals, from bugs and slugs to mice, voles, squirrels, and large deer.

19

CONIFER FORESTS

V ast forests of pines, firs, spruces, and other needle-leaved, cone-bearing trees often lack bright colors—apart from bright fungi dotting the carpet of fallen needles.

FEW INHABITANTS
In a thick conifer forest, the year-round layer of evergreen leaves high above casts a permanent shade on the ground. The fallen needles decay slowly and contain a lot of acid. So, compared to broad-leaved woods, there are few bushes, ferns, mosses, and flowers. In this habitat, fungi are often the main signs of life on the tree trunks and forest floor. Many fungi grow in close partner-ship with the roots of certain trees.

SLIPPERY JACK
Suillus luteus *gets its name from its slimy brown cap. It*
grows among the roots of conifers, especially pine trees.

LOTS OF EARS

Black ear fungus Auricularia polytricha, *also called cloud ear or mouse ear, is used in traditional Asian medicine.*

SAPROBES

Fungi are detritivores, also called scavengers or saprobes. They feed on dead and decaying matter known as detritus. In conifer woods, fungi recycle more than 80 percent of all once-living material. Other detritivores, such as worms, millipedes, insects, and microscopic bacteria, recycle the rest.

FALSE FUNGI

False chanterelle Hygrophoropsis aurantiaca *has a funnel-shaped cap and is common in conifer woods.*

LITTLE NIBBLERS

Deermice are just a few of the many creatures that nibble fungi, especially in winter, when other food sources are scarce. It is often possible to tell the identity of a fungus feeder by the shape and size of the bite marks on the cap.

THE MUSHROOM THAT "WEEPS"

The reddish-orange cap can grow to 6 inches (15 cm) across.

The red pine mushroom, *Lactarius deliciosus*, also called the saffron milk cap, has spread to many regions of the world. It followed its host trees, mostly various types of pines. The caps come in a variety of shapes and sizes. Some milk cap mushrooms produce a milky, saplike liquid when fresh. In the saffron milk cap, the color of the liquid varies from pale yellow to deep orange-red.

Saffron milk cap changes its cap shape as it emerges from the soil and matures.

BRACKETS

Brackets, conks, and shelf fungi lack a proper stalk. They grow mostly on trees—whether the tree is dead or alive.

SIGN OF AGE
Bracket fungi have flattened fruiting bodies with a round or wavy-edged shape. They usually grow

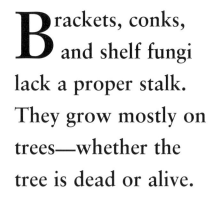

horizontally, like shelves or parts of dinner plates fixed to the tree. Their mycelia extend under the bark and into the wood. When a tree has many bracket fungi, it might be old or dying.

CLUMPS
Certain types of bracket fungi, such as the cheese bracket Tyromyces, *produce fruiting bodies in overlapping clumps.*

TINDER BRACKET
Also known as horse-hoof fungus, Fomes fomentarius *smolders for hours after burning. It was once used as tinder for fires.*

DEAD WOOD
Old, dead wood is ideal for bracket fungi. The fruiting bodies do not have ridges on the underside that release the spores. They have small holes or pores that give off spores. This is why some bracket fungi are known as polypores.

STRONG AND LONG-LASTING
Many bracket fungi are leathery and very strong. They are sometimes tougher than the tree they grow on. Some species only live for one season. Others enlarge year after year, forming colored lines similar to the growth rings in a tree trunk.

FUNGAL ROOTS
Spreading like plant roots, the fungal mycelium branches into the wood to absorb nutrition.

BEEFSTEAK FUNGUS

Brackets are basidiomycete fungi, and most are members of the polypore subgroup. However, the beefsteak *Fistulina hepatica* is a type of agaric. Also

called ox-tongue fungus, it looks similar to fresh meat. Its taste is meaty, too, but it is more sour than real steak. It grows on many trees, from oaks to eucalyptus.

When freshly cut, the beefsteak bracket may ooze a reddish, bloodlike liquid.

SADDLES AND EARS

Saddle mushrooms include types of Polyporus and Helvella (above). Like the various kinds of ear fungi Auricularia (below right), they have wavy shapes and grow directly from the wood, rather than being held up by a central stem beneath.

CHICKENS AND HENS

Relatively few bracket fungi taste good, and often they lack the typical "mushroom" flavor. They include chicken of the woods Laetiporus (below) and hen of the woods Grifola (right).

BLUSHER

The blusher Daedaleopsis confragosa has pale flesh on the fruiting body (right) that turns red or brown when rubbed. Its upper surface develops a unique pattern with age (below).

23

HIDDEN WORLD

Much of the everyday life of a fungus is hidden from our eyes. The networks of threadlike hyphae grow between and into living or dead matter, digesting nutrients as they go. We only notice the fungus when it is breeding time.

ON THE DUNG HEAP
Some of the busiest places for fungi are dung heaps and backyard compost piles.

MAKING SPORES
The common soil fungus Trichoderma *produces spores at the tips of specialized hyphae called conidiophores.*

THE MYCELIUM
The tangle of mycelia extends wherever there are nutrients and moisture. Most hyphae are thinner than hair. In some fungi, they form nutrient-carrying bundles called mycelial cords or rhizomorphs. They are thicker than a finger.

GIANTS IN TIME
In suitable soil, the mycelia continue growing year after year, covering huge areas. In Oregon, one specimen of honey fungus, *Armillaria ostoyae*, is thought to cover more than 2,000 acres (800 hectares) and be more than 8,000 years old. It is one of the world's biggest and oldest living things.

FUNGAL SPAGHETTI
A microscopic view of hyphal threads shows how they lengthen at the tips. The material in which they feed and grow has been removed.

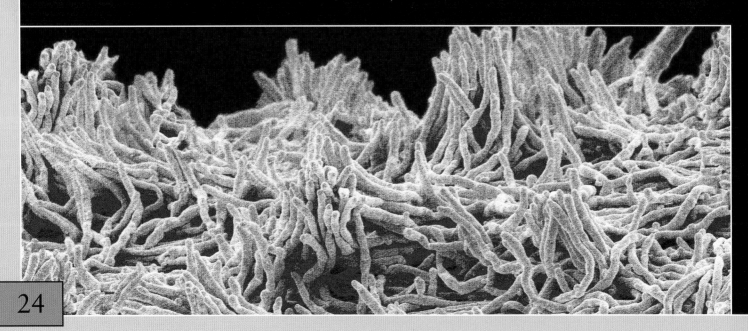

MAKING SPORE PRINTS

Spore prints are used to identify various fungi. A fresh cap is placed on paper of a different color while millions of spores fall from the gills onto it. The spores are so light that any air currents blow them around. A bowl over the cap helps prevent this. The colors of spores and the patterns they make vary among species.

Spore prints can be taken from most mushrooms. The Old Man of the Woods mushroom has a unique pattern.

HOW FUNGI REPRODUCE

Many fungi produce spores from their fruiting bodies, called hyphae, by simple cell division. The new fungus that grows from the spore is a clone—it has the same DNA as the parent fungus. In other cases, hyphae from two fungi of the same species join and form fruiting bodies. The spores have different combinations of genetic material from the parents.

SPORE-BURST
The ascomycete fungi called truffles (below) release their spores from a rounded chamber, the cleistothecium.

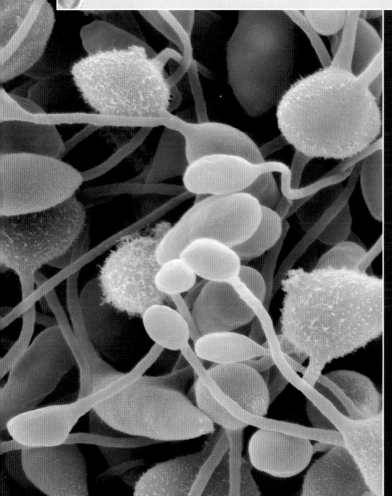

SHOOTING OUT SPORES
The spores of some fungi fall and blow away in the wind. But many basidiospores (above), from basidiomycete fungi, are thrown out with force as if on tiny springs.

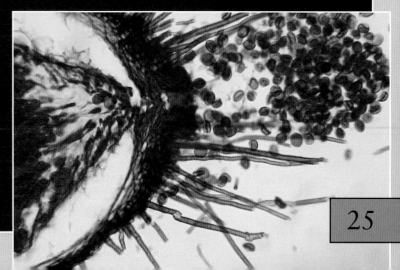

ONE CELL ONLY

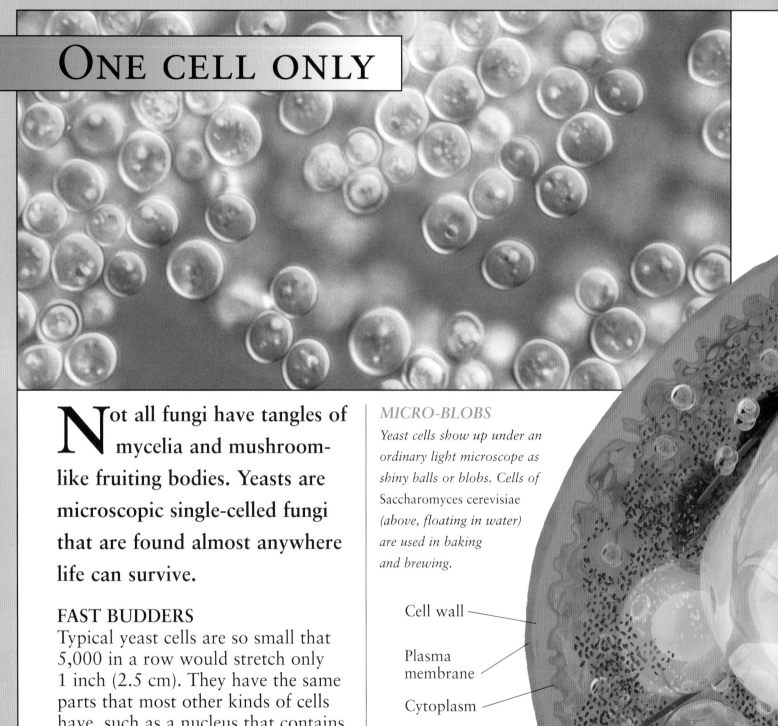

Not all fungi have tangles of mycelia and mushroom-like fruiting bodies. Yeasts are microscopic single-celled fungi that are found almost anywhere life can survive.

FAST BUDDERS

Typical yeast cells are so small that 5,000 in a row would stretch only 1 inch (2.5 cm). They have the same parts that most other kinds of cells have, such as a nucleus that contains the DNA. Yeasts multiply by budding—one end of the cell enlarges and pinches off, carrying copies of all the cell parts inside it.

YEAST PRODUCTS

There are many kinds of yeast-based foods, including the popular Australian spread Vegemite.

MICRO-BLOBS

Yeast cells show up under an ordinary light microscope as shiny balls or blobs. Cells of Saccharomyces cerevisiae (above, floating in water) are used in baking and brewing.

Cell wall

Plasma membrane

Cytoplasm

Secretory vesicles

INSIDE THE YEAST CELL

Secretory vesicles contain chemicals that break down substances on which the yeast feeds. Inside storage vacuoles are the results of digestion. Mitochondria provide energy for the cell's life processes.

Bud scar

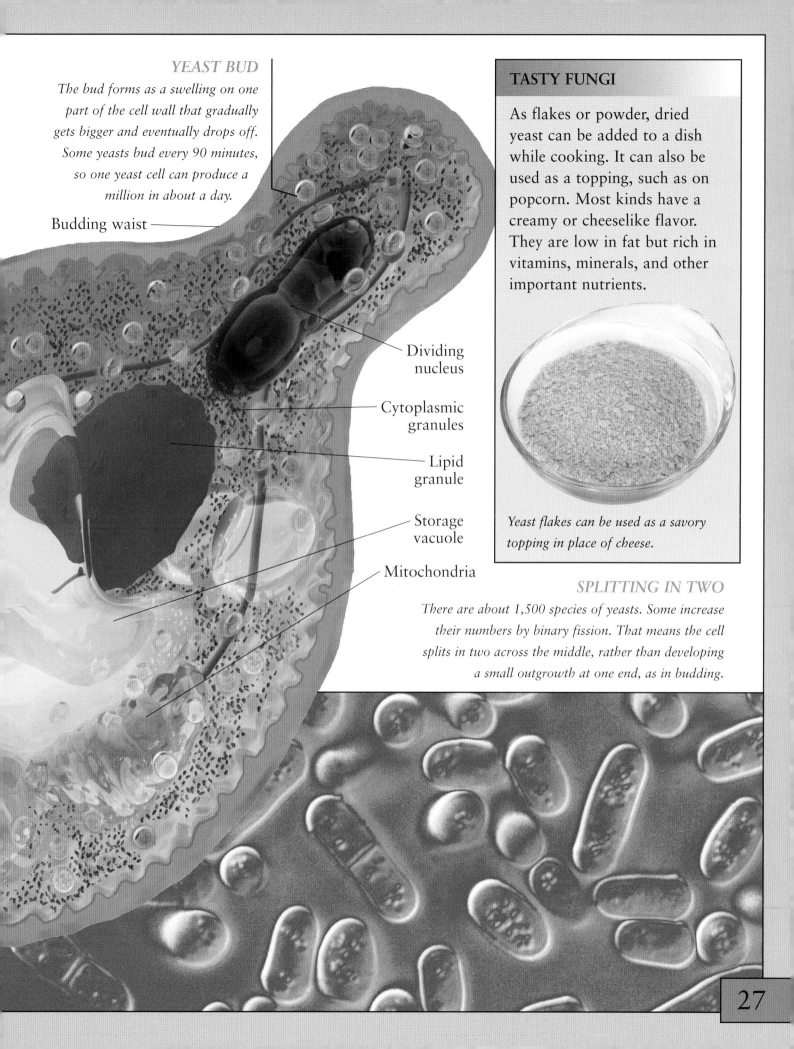

The bud forms as a swelling on one part of the cell wall that gradually gets bigger and eventually drops off. Some yeasts bud every 90 minutes, so one yeast cell can produce a million in about a day.

Budding waist

Dividing nucleus

Cytoplasmic granules

Lipid granule

Storage vacuole

Mitochondria

TASTY FUNGI

As flakes or powder, dried yeast can be added to a dish while cooking. It can also be used as a topping, such as on popcorn. Most kinds have a creamy or cheeselike flavor. They are low in fat but rich in vitamins, minerals, and other important nutrients.

Yeast flakes can be used as a savory topping in place of cheese.

SPLITTING IN TWO

There are about 1,500 species of yeasts. Some increase their numbers by binary fission. That means the cell splits in two across the middle, rather than developing a small outgrowth at one end, as in budding.

HELPFUL PARTNERS

Some fungi commonly grow with other living things, especially plantlike algae or bacteria. In this kind of relationship, called symbiosis, both partners benefit.

LIVING TOGETHER
In a lichen, the fungus digests nutrients around it into simple minerals, which are taken up by itself and the alga. Its hyphal threads protect the algal cells as well. In return, the alga makes energy-rich substances using sunlight and shares them with the fungus.

LICHENS
A lichen is a combination of fungus growing with a plantlike life-form that carries out photosynthesis—it captures energy from sunlight. In some lichens, the photosynthetic partner is a simple "plant" called an alga, from the protist group. In others it is a type of cyanobacterium, also known as a blue-green alga.

FOLIOSE LICHEN

Lichens can be crustose (in crusty layers), foliose (leaflike) or fruticose (branching).

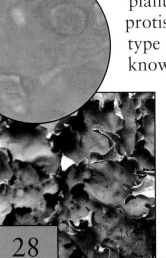

MIXED TOGETHER

The foliose lichen (left) is a fungus combined with microscopic single cells of a cyanobacterium (above left). The thallus—main body— of a rock lichen (right) contains a network of fungal hyphae.

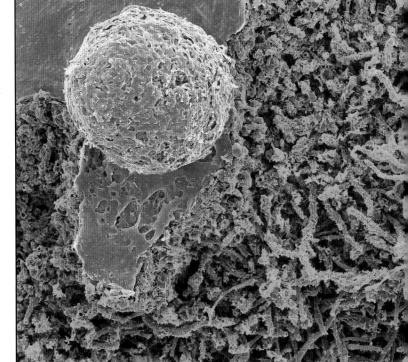

REINDEER MOSS

Reindeer moss has a fruticose (branching) growth. It can cope with being dried out or frozen solid.

Cladonia rangiferina grows as mini-forests in many cold regions, including the far north and on mountain peaks. Known as reindeer moss or caribou moss, it is not a true moss—which is a plant—but a type of lichen. It is a valuable food source for animals and people. There are more than 20,000 species of lichen worldwide.

Caribou and many other Arctic grazers rely on lichens, especially as winter approaches.

COPING WITH POLLUTION

Plenty of lichens on rocks and trees usually indicate clean air. Certain kinds die without clean air and are sometimes used as pollution detectors.

OLD AND SLOW

Depending on the conditions, lichens can grow very slowly, even less than 1 inch (2.5 cm) every 100 years. However, they can survive natural disasters such as floods, droughts, and even fires. The oldest lichens are estimated to be more than 4,000 years old.

ROCK TRIPE

Umbilicaria *lichen is used in cooking and as a medicine, especially in Asia.*

MAKING MORE LICHENS

The bright red tips of soldier lichen Cladonia cristatella are its fruiting bodies. Like fungi, they make and release spores that blow away in the wind or get carried away by water.

29

TASTY FUNGI

Widely grown is Agaricus bisporus, *known as the table, button, field, or portobello mushroom.*

A ll around the world, fungi make marvelous meals. Some kinds are not only very tasty, but also very costly.

EDIBLE FUNGI

Many traditional recipes use mushrooms and other fungi that grow in a particular region. Some examples are *shimeji* (Japan), *huitlacoche* (Mexico), Kalahari truffles (Africa), *huhtansieni* morels (Finland), wild white *callampa* (South America), and wood-ear fungi and *enokidake* (Asia).

KING BOLETE

Boletus edulis *has various names, including porcini. It is usually found among pine, spruce, fir, and oak trees. A large specimen can weigh more than 2 pounds (900 grams).*

FARMING FUNGI

Edible fungi are usually farmed in sheds or plastic tunnels. With suitable conditions of soil, temperature, light, and moisture, the fruiting bodies continually produce spores and new crops keep growing. Types include ear fungus, button and oyster mushrooms, and *shiitake* (oak mushroom).

White, button, or table mushrooms are grown on compost manure that has been treated to remove diseases.

MUSHROOM CUISINE

Fungi can be combined with many other ingredients, including cheese, rice, and various meats. A plate of stuffed mushrooms with garlic, onions, and herbs is a nutritious vegetarian meal.

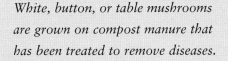

IN THE WILD

Wild fungus should always be identified to make sure it is not poisonous. After it is identified, it can be prepared as food. Many kinds of fungi are boiled, grilled, or fried. Others are dried for storage and later used as toppings. Truffles are commonly used in cooking. White truffles weighing more than 3 pounds (1.35 kg) have sold for hundreds of thousands of dollars.

STRONG FLAVOR

The aniseed fungus Clitocybe odora *gives a strong smell and taste to any dish.*

CHOICE PICKS

Various kinds of Morchella *(left) taste like fish, chicken, or nuts.* Blewits, Clitocybe, *such as the purple wood blewit (right), come in various colors. They have a flowery smell and a slightly bitter flavor. These fungi should never be eaten raw.*

YELLOWFOOT

Known as winter mushrooms, yellowfoot, or yellowlegs, Craterellus tubaeformis *is one of many types of chanterelles. It is often made into a mushroom soup.*

TRUFFLES

Truffles are lumpy underground fungi of the Tuber *group. They grow among tree roots. Certain dogs and pigs can be trained to sniff out and unearth truffles.*

DEADLY FUNGI

Great care is needed when picking wild fungi to eat. Some of the edible types look similar to some of the most poisonous species.

FUNGI POISONS

Some fungi produce poisons that affect various body parts. For example, chemicals called amatoxins in the *Amanita* fungi, such as the death cap, affect the liver and kidneys. The fly agaric's toxins cause drooling, twitching, sweating, and strange behavior, such as seeing and hearing things. The fasciculol poisons in the sulfur tuft damage the stomach and intestines, causing vomiting and diarrhea.

DEATH CAP

The yellow-green color is one way of spotting the death cap Amanita phalloides. *In many parts of the world, this mushroom causes more illness and death than any other fungus. Eating a single mushroom can result in death.*

SULFUR TUFT

Also called the clustered woodlover, Hypholoma fasciculare *grows in clumps on old or dead wood. It has a bitter taste, and its toxins can be deadly.*

LAUGHING JIM

Gymnopilus junonius (G. spectabilis), also called laughing Jim, is no laughing matter. This dangerous fungus grows in a variety of colors, from white to deep brown or dark orange. It is easily mistaken for harmless kinds.

DEATH BY FUNGI

Through the ages, deadly fungi have been given to people to harm or kill them. Because it would take time for the poison to take effect, the killer would rarely be linked to the crime. The fungus was usually slipped unnoticed into the victim's food.

Many people through history have died from eating fungi or their juices. Emperor Claudius of ancient Rome (left) may have been poisoned by the death cap (right).

MISTAKEN IDENTITIES

Some *Agaricus* fungi, such as the yellow stainer *Agaricus xanthodermus*, affect the stomach and intestines. They cause pain, vomiting, and diarrhea. But related species, such as the horse mushroom (*Agaricus arvensis*) and field mushroom (*Agaricus campestris*), are edible. However, it is best to avoid wild mushrooms unless they are identified by an expert.

STINKHORNS

The stinkhorn fungi, known as the phallales, are well named. These fungi have a strong, unpleasant odor. The group includes the Mutinus elegans *(above right),* Phallus impudicens *(right), and the starfish stinkhorn* Aseroë rubra *(below right). The smell attracts flies to spread the spores.*

ANGEL OF DEATH

Several types of pure white Amanita *fungi (above) are known as death angels. They include* Amanita bisporigera *and* Amanita virosa. *They are difficult to distinguish from edible* Amanita *species. For example, when they are newly formed, they look like puffballs (above right).*

HOME INVADER

The flowerpot parasol Lepiota lutea *is poisonous. It can spread to new regions as spores on houseplants or in the plants' soil.*

BEEFSTEAK MOREL

Resembling a brain, Gyromitra esculenta *is one of the false morel mushrooms. It can be harmful even if cooked.*

BAKING AND BREWING

For thousands of years, yeasts have been used to bake bread, brew beer, and ferment wine.

SUGAR AS FOOD

In baking, brewing, and fermenting, yeasts feed on sugary substances, which are high in energy. The yeast takes in the sugar and uses it for growing, breeding, and other life processes. As this happens, the yeast gives off carbon dioxide. Carbon dioxide makes beer fizzy and creates holes in bread as it rises.

BREADMAKING

Yeasts (left) are available as powders or pastes (above). In breadmaking they feed on the dough's starches and sugars and produce carbon dioxide, which makes the bread light and soft.

LOUIS PASTEUR

Using a specially designed glass flask (right), Louis Pasteur (1822–1895) discovered why beer and wine sometimes become sour.

Before the microscope, people knew nothing of yeasts. They thought that baking and brewing happened as chemical processes, without the need for any life-forms. In the 1850s, French scientist Louis Pasteur showed that yeasts were responsible.

DAILY BREAD

Sourdough (above) is made with partly left-over dough that already contains yeast. For most other types of bread, special types of yeasts are added. The most common type is Saccharomyces cerevisiae. Yeasts are also used when making other foods, such as buns and cakes.

WINES

Wines are alcoholic drinks made from grapes by fermentation. In this process, yeasts feed on sugars and other substances in the crushed grapes, producing carbon dioxide and alcohol. Sometimes the yeasts used are already present on the grapes as a powder. In other cases, particular species of yeasts are added to make certain types of wine.

FERMENTING

As grape juice ferments into wine, conditions such as temperature are closely controlled. Otherwise the wrong types of fungi might grow and spoil the wine so it tastes sour.

BREWING

Most types of beer are brewed by fermenting yeast with cereal grains, usually barley. The barley is malted— allowed to start growing—so that the starches in the grains turn into sugars. Then yeasts take in the sugars. This creates alcohol and a foamy layer of carbon dioxide bubbles (above). Kombucha (right) is a type of tea that is fermented into a beerlike drink using a combination of yeasts and bacteria.

ANCIENT BEER

Beer-making was well-organized in ancient Egypt, more than 4,000 years ago (below). Its history goes back more than 8,000 years in West Asia.

WINE TASTING

There are thousands of varieties of wines. Testing them by smell and taste is a great skill that takes many years of practice.

FUNGI IN THE LAB

Fungi do not grow only in nature or on mushroom farms. They are also raised and studied by biologists and other scientists in laboratories around the world.

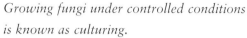

CULTURED FUNGI

Growing fungi under controlled conditions is known as culturing.

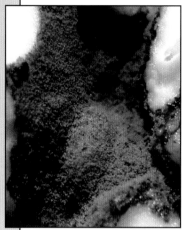

GREEN MOLD

Various types of Penicillium mold grow in soil, on rotting plants, and on old food.

MYCOLOGY

Mycologists, experts on fungi, study how fungi breed, how they take in nutrients, and which plants or animals they grow on. This is important work. Fungal diseases cause millions of dollars' worth of damage to food crops. They also cause suffering in people and animals. Finding out more about fungi helps scientists learn how to prevent or treat diseases caused by fungi.

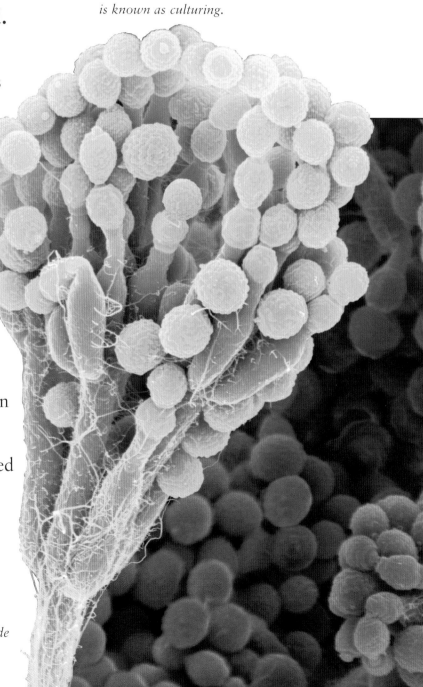

MODEL MOLD

The bread mold Neurospora crassa *is commonly used in studies because it can be easily grown.*

BREEDING PENICILLIUM

Penicillin mold multiplies and spreads by spores made on specialized stalks known as conidiophores.

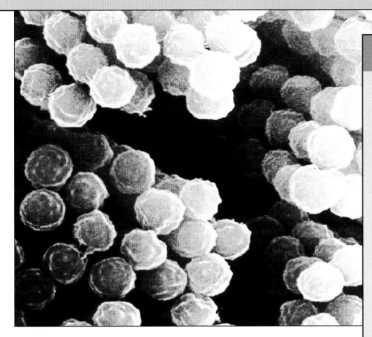

ASPERGILLUS SPORES

Several types of Aspergillus cause diseases. They are grown under strict conditions in laboratories so they do not affect the workers. The fungi are tested to see which kinds of medical drugs can kill them.

SAVING MILLIONS

One of the greatest medical advances was the discovery of penicillin, a substance made naturally by the common soil mold *Penicillium chrysogenum* (also known as *Penicillium notatum*). Since the 1940s, it has been used as an antibiotic drug to kill bacteria that infect people. Penicillin and similar fungus-based drugs have saved millions of lives.

MASS PRODUCTION

Penicillin is one of many substances made by the Penicillium mold during its life processes. The mold is continuously grown in a mixture of nutrients and other chemicals in huge tanks called bioreactors.

A HAPPY ACCIDENT

In 1928 Scottish scientist Alexander Fleming forgot to cover one of the dishes he used for growing microbes. On returning from vacation, he noticed that the dish was moldy—and the mold had killed the harmful bacteria that were supposed to grow on it. The mold was *Penicillium*. His finding led to the development of the antibiotic penicillin.

Alexander Fleming (1881–1955)

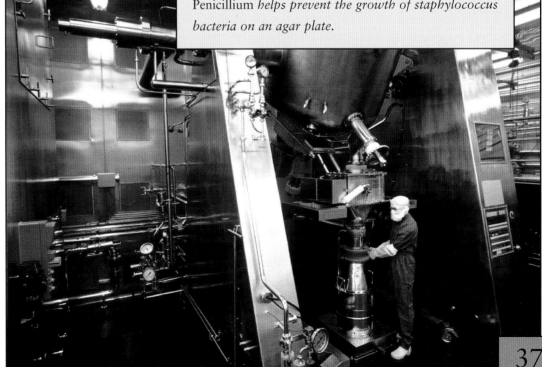

Penicillium *helps prevent the growth of staphylococcus bacteria on an agar plate.*

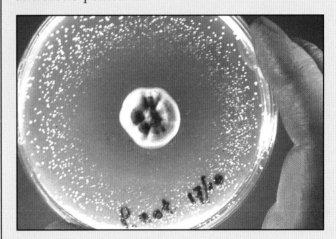

FUNGI ATTACK PLANTS

Many fungi feed on dying and dead organisms. But others attack living things. Most plants are open to infections and diseases caused by fungi.

MILDEW
Powdery mildews are caused by Erysiphales fungi, such as Erysephe. *The mycelium forms a dustlike layer on the surface.*

FUNGAL ASSAULT
Plant-infecting fungi have many common names, including rusts, mildews, cankers, and spots. Some grow as fine powders. Others form patches or lumps. These fungi can cause a large problem for fields, greenhouses, and fruit orchards. They can spread rapidly and wipe out an entire crop.

EARLY INFECTION
An enlarged view of an apple tree leaf shows apple scab Venturia *spores within the leaf starting to grow and push their hyphal threads above the surface.*

CANKERS
A plant canker is an area where living tissue has died and hardened. Cankers are commonly seen on bushes and trees as bare, dead patches like open wounds (above). Each kind of tree or bush has its own types of canker. Most are caused by a particular fungus, like Nectria Canker (left), while some are caused by bacteria.

FUNGI OR WITCHCRAFT?

In the 1690s, about 150 people were arrested in and around Salem, Massachusetts. Their odd behavior, with screaming, fits, and seeing or hearing things, led to accusations of witchcraft. Some people believe the cause was a poisonous fungus from damp rye crops in their bread.

Rye fungus Claviceps *contains ergot poisons.*

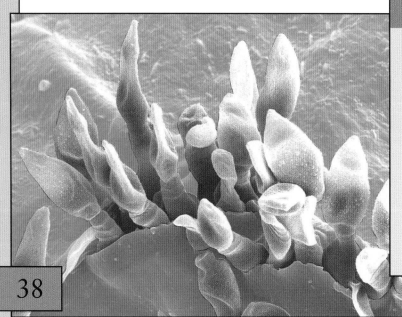

UNWANTED GUESTS

Various Botrytis fungi infest many plants, from vegetables such as leeks (above) to grapes (left). Outbreaks occur when the crop is damp and the air is stale.

FIGHTING BACK

Farmers and plant growers face an ongoing battle against fungal pests. One defense is to spray pesticide chemicals such as fungicides or antifungals. But by the time the fungus infection is discovered, it may already have weakened and damaged the plants beyond recovery.

GOOD AND BAD EATERS

Huitlacoche *(right) is also known as corn smut. In some areas, it causes great damage to corn crops. It may not look tasty, but it is a traditional food in Mexico. Corn smut is valued for its earthy yet delicate flavor. It is sometimes called the Mexican truffle. The fungi that make up dry rot (below) eat away at the structure of wood, making it weak and brittle.*

ANTIFUNGALS

Chemicals that kill fungi are found in various plants and animals. Cecropin-A, which is being tested against cotton boll rot, comes from the large cecropia moth.

REGULAR SPRAYING

Many farmers pay for fungicide chemicals and sprayers to treat their crops at certain times of year, whether there are signs of fungal disease or not. It is difficult to predict outbreaks of infections such as soybean rust (inset).

Nineteen people were sentenced to hang during the Salem witch trials.

FUNGI ATTACK ANIMALS

Fungal diseases of animals do not only cause suffering in wild creatures, livestock, and pets. Some of them can also be passed on to people.

THREAT TO LIFE

Aspergillus is one of the most varied groups of fungi. Certain species infest plants, animals, and humans. In animals the fungus often grows in the breathing passages to produce sniffing, coughing, panting, and fever. This is known as respiratory aspergillosis. If the animal becomes weaker, perhaps from another illness, the fungal mycelium may start growing into its body, which may result in death.

DEAD DUCKS

Some of the effects of aspergillosis in birds can be similar to the deadly H5N1 strain of the virus infection known as avian influenza or the bird flu. In 2006 more than 2,500 mallard ducks (top) died in Idaho. This sparked fears of a huge outbreak of the bird flu. Tests on the ducks' inner parts, including the lungs (above), showed that the disease was a form of aspergillosis from eating grains moldy with fungus.

MANY ANIMALS

Coccidioides *causes a rash and influenza-like illness in humans and many animals, including apes, monkeys, cows, llamas, tigers, bears, and seals. It occurs in southern North America and is known as San Joaquin Valley fever or coccidioidomycosis.*

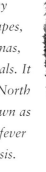

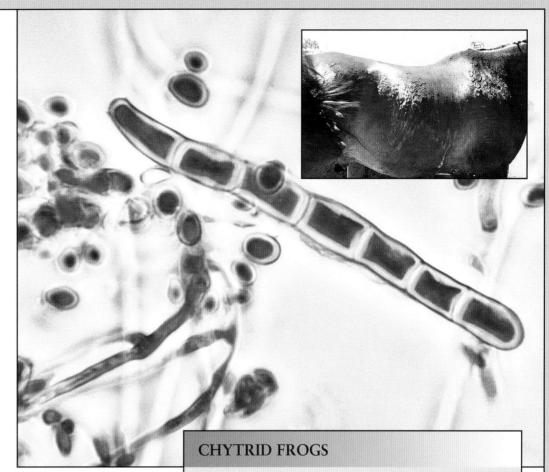

ITCHY RING

Horses (inset) are among the many animals that catch ringworm. The tinea type of fungus (right) grows from a central area, forming a raised red ring that slowly widens. The skin within the ring gradually heals.

RINGWORM

Tinea, also called ringworm, causes ring-shaped rashes or patches on the skin of people and animals. However, it is not due to a worm, but to a variety of fungi.

SNIFFING TROUBLE

Blastomycosis is caused by the mold Blastomyces dermatitidis. *It commonly affects dogs that are in the countryside often, where they breathe in spores from the soil. Signs include coughing, fever, skin rash, eye disease, and a general lack of energy.*

CHYTRID FROGS

Frogs, toads, salamanders, and other amphibians in many parts of the world have been devastated by chytridiomycosis. It is caused by *Batrachochytrium dendrobatidis*, a type of chytrid fungus. The first infections were reported in the 1990s. Since then more than 90 percent of frogs in some areas have died. The fungus spreads by spores that have "tails" that allow them to swim in water.

In frogs with chytrid disease, the skin becomes rough and peels away. The legs stick out straight and cannot bend at the joints or fold against the body.

41

HUMAN FUNGAL DISEASES

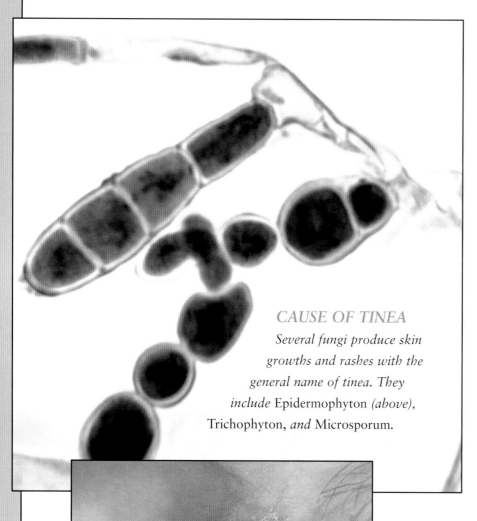

CAUSE OF TINEA

Several fungi produce skin growths and rashes with the general name of tinea. They include Epidermophyton *(above),* Trichophyton, *and* Microsporum.

Some of the fungal diseases that affect people date back to ancient times. Others are more recent, with outbreaks possibly caused by modern chemicals and pollution.

CONSTANT EXPOSURE
Fungal spores are much too small for us to see. Even in "clean" air, they land on our skin and are inhaled. A healthy body usually fights against them and stops them from growing. But if a person is already ill from another disease or is taking certain kinds of medicine, then the spores may be able to germinate. The skin, nose, mouth, airways, and lungs are the parts most often affected.

TYPES OF TINEA

Tinea that affects the skin between the toes is called tinea pedis—athlete's foot (above left). It also affects the nails as onychomycosis (left), the groin as tinea cruris (jock itch), the head and scalp as tinea capitis, and the body as tinea corporis, also known as ringworm (right).

TRIVIAL OR DEADLY?

Some fungal diseases, such as athlete's foot and fungal nail infections, are irritating but not life-threatening. However, it may take weeks or months of medical treatment to get rid of the mycelia and spores completely. Other fungal diseases spread through the body in the blood. They can become much more serious, especially if they affect vital parts such as the heart or brain.

CANDIDA

Oral thrush (left, inset), which causes pale patches to grow in the mouth and throat, is caused by the yeast fungus Candida albicans. *If the same fungus gets deeper inside the body, it can grow in the heart's inner lining. Known as candida endocarditis, this complication can be fatal.*

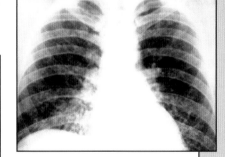

NEW ANTIFUNGALS

Medical scientists explore all kinds of sources for antifungal drugs—including other fungi. A common black mold of soil and decay, *Epicoccum*, is being tested for substances that kill bacteria and fungi that cause plant diseases.

New antifungal treatments are tested before they are sold to make sure they are safe.

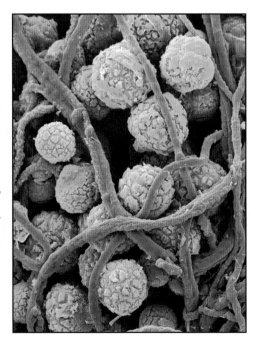

Epicoccum purpurascens

DEADLY DROPPINGS

Histoplasmosis lung disease causes a white "snowstorm" effect on lung X-rays (above). Its cause, the Histoplasma *fungus, is found in soil (right). It is also found in animal droppings, especially those left by birds and bats.*

CLASSIFICATION OF LIFE

Scientists classify living things depending on how their features and the parts inside them compare to other living things. All fungi share certain features, including the ability to make spores. Another example is the way they obtain nourishment—by digesting nutrients into simple substances outside their bodies and then absorbing the substances.

The main groups of living things are known as domains. The next groups are usually kingdom, phylum (division), class, order, family, genus, and species. To see how this system works, follow the example on page 45 of how to classify the well-known fly agaric toadstool *Amanita muscaria* within the Basidiomycota (Basidiomycetes) phylum of the Fungi kingdom.

BIOLOGICAL CLASSIFICATION: DOMAINS

BACTERIA

Single-celled prokaryotes, found in most places on Earth

ARCHAEA

Single-celled prokaryotes, many surviving in extreme conditions

EUKARYA

KINGDOMS

PROTISTA: Single-celled eukaryotes, with some simple multicelled forms

FUNGI: Multicelled life-forms that digest their food externally

PLANTAE: Multicelled life-forms that obtain energy by photosynthesis

ANIMALIA: Multicelled life-forms that get their energy by taking in food

Scientists split the Fungi kingdom into six to 10 phyla. The two largest by far are the ascomycotans and basidiomycotans.

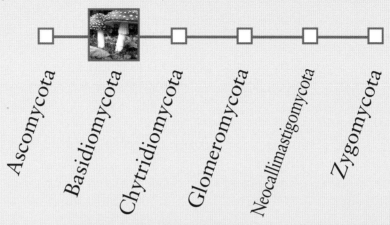

Ascomycota

Basidiomycota

Chytridiomycota

Glomeromycota

Neocallimastigomycota

Zygomycota

The fly agaric is the typical, brightly colored toadstool with a white-spotted red cap. It is found in warm to cool northern lands around the world.

KINGDOM: Fungi

PHYLUM: Basidiomycota

SUBPHYLUM: Agaricomycotina

CLASS: Agaricomycetes

ORDER: Agaricales

FAMILY: Amanitaceae

GENUS: *Amanita*

SPECIES: *muscaria*

Amanita muscaria *(Fly agaric)*

GLOSSARY

ANTIBIOTICS
Medical drugs that attack and disable or kill bacteria and similar microbes (but usually not viruses)

CELL
Basic unit, or "building block," of life; some microscopic living things, such as bacteria, are one cell each; plants, animals, and fungi have billions of cells

CELL WALL
Thick outer layer of some cells that gives the cell shape and strength

CULTURE
To grow bacteria, fungi, and similar living things in a controlled environment

CYTOPLASM
Thin watery fluid inside a cell in which various parts float and many substances are dissolved

DNA
Deoxyribonucleic acid, the chemical substance that carries genetic information about how a living thing grows and survives

EUKARYOTE
Living cell that has an outer cell membrane and other membranes inside, enclosing parts of the cell, such as the nucleus

FERMENTATION
Process of breaking apart complex substances into simple ones; yeasts are commonly used during this process to break apart sugars to produce alcohol and carbon dioxide

FRUITING BODY
Part of a fungus or similar living thing that produces the spores; commonly known as the mushroom or toadstool in fungi

GERMINATE
When a plant seed, spore, or similar part starts to develop after reaching suitable conditions of light, moisture, and nutrients

HYPHAE
Individual threads of the mycelium that forms the main body of some living things, such as water molds and many fungi

MITOCHONDRIA
Tiny sausage-shaped parts inside a cell that break apart nutrients from food to get energy

MYCELIA
Tangled, threadlike network forming the main body of some living things, such as water molds and fungi

MYCORRHIZAE
Rootlike structures formed by the symbiotic relationship between a fungus and the roots of a plant

NUCLEUS
Control center of a living cell; contains DNA and is surrounded by a nuclear membrane

PHOTOSYNTHESIS
Process of capturing light energy to join simple substances and create food, which is used to grow, develop, and carry out life processes

PILEUS
Wide upper part of a fungal fruiting body, which is often umbrella-shaped; also called a cap

PLASMA MEMBRANE
Thin covering or skin of a living cell

PROKARYOTE
Living cell that has a cell membrane covering but no separate membranes inside; it lacks membrane-enclosed parts, such as a nucleus

RHIZOMORPHS
Thick, rootlike parts of a fungal mycelium that consist of bundles of many hyphae

STIPE
Stalk or stem of a fungal fruiting body that holds the cap (pileus) above the mycelium, as in mushrooms and toadstools

SPORES
Single microscopic cells usually used during asexual reproduction; each spore lies in a tough casing for protection

SYMBIOSIS
When two species of living things exist closely together; both species benefit from the partnership

VACUOLE
Pool or blob of a substance, such as water, nutrients, or waste products, inside a living cell

VOLVA
Cuplike container at the base of the stalk or stem of a mushroom or toadstool fruiting body; also called a basal cap

Look for all the books in this series:

FURTHER RESOURCES

FURTHER READING

King, Katie, and Jacqueline A. Ball, eds. *Protists and Fungi*. Milwaukee: Gareth Stevens Publishing, 2003.

Pascoe, Elaine. *Fungi*. New York: PowerKids Press, 2003.

Silverman, Buffy. *Molds and Fungi*. San Diego: Kidhaven Press, 2004.

Snedden, Robert. *Plants and Fungi: Multicelled Life*. Chicago: Heinemann Library, 2007.

INTERNET SITES
FactHound offers a safe, fun way to find Internet sites related to this book. All of the sites on FactHound have been researched by our staff.

Here's all you do:

Visit *www.facthound.com*

FactHound will fetch the best sites for you!

INDEX